INTIMACY

Living
THE GOOD LIFE
TOGETHER

INTIMACY
pursuing love

study & reflection guide

M. Garlinda Burton

ABINGDON PRESS / Nashville

LIVING THE GOOD LIFE TOGETHER
INTIMACY: PURSUING LOVE
Study & Reflection Guide

Copyright © 2007 by Abingdon Press

Scripture quotations in this publication, unless otherwise indicated, are from the New Revised Standard Version of the Bible, copyrighted © 1989 by the Division of Christian Education of the National Council of the Churches of Christ in the United States of America, and are used by permission.

This book is printed on acid-free, elemental chlorine-free paper.

ISBN 978-0-687-64384-4

07 08 09 10 11 12 13 14 15 16—10 9 8 7 6 5 4 3 2 1
MANUFACTURED IN THE UNITED STATES OF AMERICA

Contents

—1—

An Introduction to This Study Series

PSALM FOR PRAYING

Psalm 139:1-3

O LORD, you have searched me and known me.
You know when I sit down and when I rise up;
   you discern my thoughts from far away.
You search out my path and my lying down,
   and are acquainted with all my ways.

CHRISTIAN CHARACTER IN COMMUNITY

THE GREAT EARLY Christian theologian Augustine opens his *Confessions* with these famous words: "Restless is our heart until it comes to rest in thee." Augustine, who had himself led a life of distorted and disordered desires that left him frustrated and without satisfaction, eventually discovered that we only find satisfaction when we rest in God. We are created for life with God, and only through God's love will we discover the rest, wholeness, and fullness we most truly desire.

So how can we discover this fullness of life that we yearn for, especially when we try and try but can't seem to get any satisfaction? Ironically, we will only discover it when we quit trying so hard. Instead, we need to learn to rest in God, the God who loves us and embraces us before we can do anything. God's grace invites us to discover that we cannot earn love; we can only discover it in the gift of being loved.

So far, so good. But it seems easier said than done. After all, to receive the gift of being loved calls for us to love in return. And yet we lack the skills—and often the desire—to love in the way God loves us. As a result, as wonderful as it sounds to "rest in God," to discover "the gift of being loved by God," we fear that we are not up to the relationship.

In order to truly receive love, we want to become like the lover. So for us to truly receive God's love, we are called to become like God—and that sounds both inviting and scary. Become like God? This becomes even more daunting when we discover that this gracious, loving God is also the one who is called "holy" and calls us through God's love to be holy as well. Jesus even enjoins us to be "perfect" as our "heavenly Father is perfect" (Matthew 5:48). The task begins to seem overwhelming. How does this relate to the idea of resting in God's grace?

The wonder and joy of Christian life is that we are invited by God into a way of life, a life of abundance in which we learn to cultivate habits of desiring, thinking, feeling, and living that continually open us to the grace of God's holiness. The invitation to Christian life is an invitation to discover that "the good life" is lived in the light of God's grace. When we embark on a truly Christian life, we learn to become holy not by trying really hard but by continually being drawn into the disciplined habits of living as friends of God in the community of others.

This may seem odd at first, but think about it in terms of learning to play the piano. We're drawn by the desire to play beautiful music. But before we can play beautiful music, we have to learn basic habits: the position of our hands, the scales of the piano, the role of the foot pedals, and the rhythms of music. Over time, as we learn these basic skills, our teachers invite us to take on more challenging tasks. Eventually, we find ourselves playing with both hands, learning to master more complicated arrangements of music, and perhaps even integrating the foot pedals into our playing. If we practice the piano long enough, we will reach a point where it seems effortless to play—and even to improvise new music—in the company of others.

It's around this metaphor of practice that Living the Good Life Together: A Study of Christian Character in Community has been developed. Rather than to practice being piano players, this series of small-group studies is aimed at helping persons practice being Christian. Each unit of study is designed to move persons from *understanding* various aspects of Christian character to the development of *practices* reflective of those aspects of Christian character to, ultimately, the *embodiment* of Christian character in community. In other words, the idea is to educate the desires of heart and mind in order to develop, over time, patterns of living like Christ.

A billboard or bumper sticker would say it more succinctly: "The Good Life: Get It. Try It. Live It—Together."

Living the Good Life Together gets at the heart of the life God intends for us, particularly as it relates to others in community. Attentiveness, forgiveness, discernment, intimacy, humility, hospitality—these are some of the aspects of the life God intends for us. And they are the subjects of this study series.

STUDY FORMAT

The overall process of this study series is based on some of Jesus' own words to his followers: "Come and see" (John 1:39) and "Go and do likewise" (Luke 10:37). In each study, the first six sessions are the backbone of the "Come and See" portion. These sessions inspire and teach the group about a particular character trait of the Christian life. The second six sessions are the "Go and Do" portion. For these sessions, the study offers tools to help group members plan how to put into practice what they have learned.

"Come and See"

Session 1: An Introduction to This Study Series

This session is an orientation to the twelve-week study. It provides information about the Living the Good Life Together series and an introduction to the trait of Christian character addressed in that particular study.

Sessions 2–5: Topics in Christian Character

These sessions offer information about aspects of the particular trait of Christian character. The sessions will help group members explore the trait and will foster intimacy with Scripture, with others, and with God.

Session 6: Planning the Next Steps Together

In this session, group members plan what they will do together in Sessions 7–12 to practice the Christian character trait they have learned about in the previous sessions.

"Go and Do"

Sessions 7–12: From Study to Practice

In these sessions, group members will carry out their plans from Session 6, putting their learnings into practice.

USING THE RESOURCE COMPONENTS

The resource components of Living the Good Life Together—the study & reflection guide, leader guide, and DVD—and the group sessions function together to foster intimacy with Scripture, with others, and with God. This takes place through a broad range of approaches: reading, writing, discussion, viewing video, prayer, worship, and practical application.

Study & Reflection Guide

This book serves as a guide for individual preparation from week to week, as a personal journal for responding to all elements of the study, and as a planning tool for the "Go and Do" portion of the study. Becoming familiar with the following content sections will enhance the effectiveness of this guide.

Psalm for Praying

A psalm text appears on the first page of each session of the study & reflection guide. It is there for you to use as a prayer of invocation as you begin your study each day.

Daily Readings

Reading these passages each day is central to your preparation for the group meeting. Consider reading from different translations of the Bible to hear familiar texts in a fresh way. Ask what the Scriptures mean in light of the session's theme and how they apply

11

to your own life. Be alert to insights and questions you would like to remember for the group meeting, and jot those down in the boxes provided in this study & reflection guide.

Reflections

The space at the bottom of each page in each content session of the study & reflection guide is provided for making notes or recording any thoughts or questions the reading brings to mind.

Lectio Divina

Each session of this study will include a prayer exercise called *lectio divina*, sometimes called "praying the Scriptures." The practice of lectio divina, which is Latin for "sacred reading," continues to gain popularity as people discover anew this ancient and meaningful approach to prayer.

In the practice of lectio divina outlined as follows, we listen, as the Benedictines instruct, "with the ear of the heart" for a word, phrase, sound, or image that holds a special meaning for us. This could be a word of comfort, instruction, challenge, or assurance. It could be an image suggested by a word, and the image could take us to a place of deep reverence or personal introspection.

It is important to note that like the biblical exercises in this book, lectio divina is about what is evoked in you as you experience the text. Now is not the time for historical-critical musings or scholarly interpretations of the text. It is time for falling in love with the Word and experiencing the goodness of God.

Step One: *Silencio.* After everyone has turned to the Scripture, be still. Silently turn all your thoughts and desires over to God. Let go of concerns, worries, or agendas. Just *be* for a few minutes.

Step Two: *Lectio.* Read the passage of Scripture slowly and carefully, either aloud or silently. Reread it. Be alert to any word, phrase, or image that invites you, that puzzles you, that intrigues you. Wait for this word, phrase, or image to come to you; try not to rush it.

Step Three: *Meditatio.* Take the word, phrase, or image from your Scripture passage that comes to you and ruminate over it. Repeat it to yourself. Allow this word, phrase, or image to engage your thoughts, your desires, your memories. You may share your word, phrase, or image with others in the group, but don't feel pressured to speak.

Step Four: *Oratio.* Pray that God transform you through the word, phrase, or image from Scripture. Consider how this word, phrase, or image connects with your life and how God is made known to you in it. This prayer may be either silent or spoken.

Step Five: *Contemplatio.* Rest silently in the presence of God. Move beyond words, phrases, or images. Again, just *be* for a few minutes. Close this time of lectio divina with "Amen."

(Adapted by permission from *50 Ways to Pray: Practices From Many Traditions and Times,* by Teresa A. Blythe, Abingdon Press, 2006; pages 45–47)

Faithful Friends

True friends in faith are those who can help us hear the voice of God in our lives more clearly. They act as our mentors, our guides. At times they weep with us, and at other times they laugh with us. At all times they keep watch over us in love and receive our watch-care in return. Having a faithful friend (or friends) and being a faithful friend are at the heart of what it means to live as a Christian in community for at least three reasons:

• Faithful friends can at times challenge the sins we have come to love.
• Faithful friends will affirm the gifts we are afraid to claim.
• Faithful friends help us dream the dreams we otherwise wouldn't have imagined.

During this study, each group member will be invited to join with one or two others to practice being a faithful friend over the course of the twelve weeks and hopefully beyond. While there are no "mystical" qualifications for being a faithful friend, what *is* required is the willingness to be open to possibilities of guiding another person or persons into a deeper and richer experience of Christian living. Like all aspects of the Christian life, this activity of being a faithful friend is a discipline, a practice.

A key decision faithful friends will make is how to stay in touch week after week. Some may choose to meet over lunch or coffee or take a walk. Others may choose to use e-mail or the telephone. Whatever the means, consider using the following questions to stimulate an ongoing conversation over the course of the study:

- How has it gone for you, trying to live the week's practice?
- What's been hard about it?
- What's been easy or comfortable?
- What challenges have there been? What rewards?
- What kinds of things happened this week—at work, at home, in your prayer life—that you want to talk about? Has anything affected your spiritual life and walk?

There's an old African proverb that says, "If you want to go fast, go alone. If you want to go far, go together." In the end, a faithful friend is someone who is willing to go the distance with you, following Christ all the way. The aim of this feature of the study is to move you further down the way of Christian discipleship in the company of another.

INTIMACY: PURSUING LOVE

Intimacy is the Christian character trait featured in this study of Living the Good Life Together. Intimacy, or the condition of being intimate, indicates knowledge of the innermost character of a thing, of being very familiar with someone or something. True intimacy comes through careful attention to the person or thing we seek to know, and such attention and presence calls forth effort. Because of this effort to be present and to pay attention, the thought of developing intimacy as a trait of Christian character may challenge many of us. Most of us have intimate knowledge of people in our families, in our friendships, and in our work settings. Maintaining those relationships requires time and energy. How is it possible to nurture intimacy with everyone we meet? Why do we need to know the innermost character, feelings, and thoughts of the people we meet?

Intimacy as a trait of Christian character is grounded in the Great Commandment to love God with heart, soul, strength, and mind and to love your neighbor as you love yourself (Luke 10:25-28; Matthew 22:34-40; Mark 12:28-34), teachings that were the heart of God's law (Deuteronomy 6:5; Leviticus 19:18). The practice of all three dimensions of the Great Commandment, love of God, self, and neighbor, places the practice of developing intimacy in a healthy psychological and spiritual framework. As we work at developing our intimacy with God and with ourselves, we discover that God gives us the energy and motivation to nurture intimacy with our neighbor. We also discover that developing practices that lead to intimacy sets the stage for choosing to act with compassion, justice, and mercy.

Our study of Christian intimacy begins with the almost unbelievable understanding that we are worthy of being loved—by God, by others, by ourselves. God created in us a yearning for intimacy, a deep need to be known, a desire to be at-one with God and others. As our trust in God deepens, we journey deeper into intimacy. Intimacy comes not because we deserve it, but because we need it.

Biblical writers note this miracle again and again. In John 4, Jesus had conversation with a Samaritan woman at Jacob's well, and he communicated his intimate knowledge of her life. She was astonished and announced, "Come and see a man who told me everything I have ever done! He cannot be the Messiah, can he?" Galatians 6:2 states that intimacy both comes from and results in bearing one another's burdens. Other writers confirm that God expects us to do acts of justice, mercy, and reconciliation. It is these acts that result in intimacy within the faith community and with the world, and it is the practice of attaining intimacy that nurtures these acts. Colossians urges us to clothe ourselves with compassion, kindness, humility, and other traits; these are both born of and lead to intimacy.

Jesus longed for and sought intimacy in his relationship with God, with disciples and the faith community, and with the larger world. The sessions in INTIMACY: PURSUING LOVE explore our need to become more intimate with God, with ourselves, and with others. "Knowing Who You Are—And Whose You Are" looks at what it means to be loved by God. "Seeing God's Love in Others" addresses God's yearning for intimacy. "Connecting With a Community of Faith" looks at intimacy in the congregation, in the community of faith. "Practicing Intimacy as a Spiritual Discipline" encourages deepening one's faith journey. "Planning the Next Steps Together" facilitates a group planning process for putting into practice what the group has learned about intimacy. All the sessions help us deepen our relationship with God and practice intimacy as a spiritual discipline.

—2—

Knowing Who You Are — And Whose You Are

Psalm 139:4, 13-14

> Even before a word is on my tongue,
>   O Lord, you know it completely.
>   . . .
> For it was you who formed my inward parts;
>   you knit me together in my mother's
>   womb.
> I praise you, for I am fearfully and wonder-
>   fully made.
>   Wonderful are your works.

Daily Readings

DAY ONE
Mark 12:28-34 *(The commandment to love)*

DAY TWO
Acts 20:28-32 *(Paul's exhortation to the faithful)*

DAY THREE
1 Corinthians 13:1-13 *(Love never ends)*

DAY FOUR

Romans 8:37-39 *(Nothing can separate us from God's love)*

DAY FIVE

1 Chronicles 16:31-34 *(God's steadfast love endures forever)*

DAY SIX

Read the chapter on pages 20–25. You may take notes in the space provided at the bottom of each page.

I WAS ON ASSIGNMENT in rural Nicaragua, interviewing women about their lives and their attempt to raise enough food and make enough money to feed themselves and their children. It was there that I met Maria. We had an instant spiritual connection.

As she told me the story of her struggles—not enough food, widowed at an early age by civil war and left with four children, scratching out a living as a farmer—I nonetheless noticed a lilting spirit, a certain straightness of her shoulders despite the bent-back work. Then she asked me if I was Christian, and asked me to tell her and the other women gathered about my faith.

I told my story briefly, then asked her to share. "Never," she said, "have I doubted that I am a daughter of God. Through hunger, the death of my husband, and those days when I think I cannot find the strength to go to the field, I have always known that I am blessed. God walks with me. God digs with me in the field. God rocks my babies with me. God weeps with me. I am important to God."

The other women nodded and smiled at me. Maria waved her hand to indicate the sentiment of her sisters. "We may be poor, and our feet may be dusty from plowing. But we know that God loves even the dirty feet of our children. In the name of Jesus Christ, we are precious to the Greatest One."

Intimacy and the Nature of God

In my own life, my relationship with my mother is the closest I have on earth to mirroring my relationship with God through Jesus Christ. My mother has seen me at my absolute worst: as a sullen, pimple-faced, smart-alecky teenager; as a fragile, frazzled college student; as a naïve, frightened bride; as a grumpy new

reflections

supervisor. My mother has endured my tantrums, rebellion, and questionable personal decisions. She has been with me through the joys of graduations, marriage, and career success; and she has walked with me through the hard times of my life, including the devastating death of my husband.

Through all my warts and triumphs, joys and struggles, affectations and tears, she has been unwavering in her support, her belief in my brilliance and ability, her fretting and worrying every time my travel-heavy job takes me away from home, and her continuous flow of unconditional love.

That is the nature of God, in my mind, and that is the story of Jesus and his love—knowing with unshakeable assurance that God's love is everlasting, eternal, binding, and unconditional. It is that God-love, that mother-love, that gives me confidence to take risks, try new things, work to excel, reach out to new kinds of people, and step out on faith. I have been the first woman and first person of color in several jobs, and that hasn't always been easy. But I am a child of God and the child of a mother who still tells me I can be anything I want and excel in anything I undertake.

> **God's love is everlasting, eternal, binding, and unconditional.**

Not only do I believe that about myself, I believe that all people—created in God's image—have that God-given potential. I work with inner-city kids through a program in my congregation, and many of my kids have virtually been written off by the school system, forgotten by an overwhelmed foster-care system, and warehoused by juvenile courts. But I've seen the God in them blossom and transform them. Sean went from being a sullen, angry teen who cursed teachers and put

reflections

21

his fist through a wall to being a young man earning a scholarship and thriving as a student in a prestigious, church-related college. I've seen Claudia, a listless runaway at age thirteen, grow into a sixteen-year-old honor student and featured soloist in choirs at church and in school. Why? Because these two found relationships with the God who created them as "wonderfully made" (Psalm 139:14), as the writer of this psalm writes, because the youth were embraced by adults—pastors, Sunday school teachers, parents, teachers—who had confidence in, recognized, and connected to the best part of Sean and Claudia.

CHRISTIAN CHARACTER IN CONTEXT

Intimacy is most commonly understood as a relationship between two people. Various dictionaries describe intimacy as the ultimate expression of person-to-person closeness, familiarity, and a sense of belonging together. However, I would contend that the deepest intimacies with others require one to know and love oneself, and to know and experience the sense of being loved and justified as a child of a loving God. We hear it so often from pop psychologists that it has become cliché, but it is true: You can't love and accept others until you learn to love yourself.

From the beginning, the writer of Psalm 139 emphasizes how well God knows us. You can almost imagine the psalmist smiling at the discovery: "Even before a word is on my tongue, / O Lord, you know it completely" (139:4). Such a sense of excitement and giddiness comes through the words. It is almost too much. And as we realize that feeling of being known, the next question is whether that is something that makes us excited and happy, like our

reflections

psalmist friend, or whether it is something that unnerves or even frightens us. If we are not always impressed by our own thoughts or actions, then it may not be such a comfortable feeling to learn that God knows everything about us.

The point of this psalm, however, is that God does know us and that the same all-knowing God accepts us as we are. Indeed, as recorded in Deuteronomy 6:4-6, God wants our love in return and wants us to share that love story—and the love itself—in a way that transforms our friendships, romantic relationships, family ties, community relations, and the whole world. The Great Commandment of Jesus is rooted in God's love and acceptance (Matthew 22:34-40; Mark 12:28-34; Luke 10:25-28).

Ruth Hutchison, a pastor at All Hallows Church in England, in considering Psalm 139 in a sermon (October 16, 2005), states, "One of the deep-rooted problems in our society is people's inability or unwillingness to accept and love themselves." Healing and right relationships come, says Hutchinson, when we accept the invitation "to really deepen our relationship with Christ as someone who knows us completely and loves us as we are. There are no secret sections of ourselves hidden from God. We cannot introduce ourselves to God as the person we want to be tomorrow, or next week, nor can we pretend that we are someone we are not. God knows us and loves us now, at this moment, in all our glory and in all our shame."

This is the beginning of intimacy: accepting that we are worthy to be loved simply because God loves us. Successful sisterhood, brotherhood, friendship, romantic relationships, and parent-child love all begin with the understanding held by the writer of Psalm 139: the strong belief that we are divinely made and a part of God's plan.

reflections

23

INTIMACY AND CONFLICT

If the beginning of intimacy with God is accepting that God loves us, the next step is realizing that intimacy cannot happen—with God or with anyone else—without conflict. It is conflict, and the resolution of conflict, that makes us more intimate with God. Voicing our fears, our anger, our true feelings makes us more honest with God...and opens the way for God to be more honest with us.

Conflict—saying what you really think and feel, and being open to hear what God really thinks and feels—is the deep work of intimacy. It's true in our relationships with people. The dullest relationships we have are those in which there is no honesty, no straightforward talk, no direct dealing with conflict.

It takes courage to risk intimacy, especially with God.

It's also true in our relationship with God, and Jesus is a good example of that. The Bible reports that Jesus felt challenged by God (in the wilderness), pushed emotionally by God (in the Gethsemane garden), forsaken by God (on the cross). Yet there was a resolution of these feelings, an end to the conflict, a deep intimacy between the two.

God yearns for intimacy with us, between us and our mates, among us and our family and friends. It takes courage to risk intimacy, especially with God. It takes time and energy and prayer. But God gives us the courage, the strength, the energy to do it. God also, in the Bible, gives us stories of unlikely people who dared to speak their true feelings to God, who had the courage to seek inti-

reflections

macy with God, and who changed the history of our faith, indeed the course of history.

These are people who, in spite of their own foibles and imperfections, their own doubts and fears, came to understand that God called them and loved them and created them as wonderful, unique, and even critical to the workings in God's world. Even when the rest of the world had all but written them off, God embraced them, strengthened them, and transformed them.

In Acts 9, Saul, a persecutor of Christ's followers, encountered the blinding love and power of God on the road to Damascus, and through that encounter became arguably the most prolific theologian in Christian history. When Mary learned that she was pregnant with Jesus the Christ, she gradually accepted and celebrated her God-ordained role in transforming human history (Luke 1:26-38). Joseph, who had initially decided to quietly divorce Mary when he learned she was pregnant, accepted his role as Mary's husband (Matthew 1:18-24). The adulterer David, the woman at the well, Peter who denied knowing Jesus—all these biblical characters had glaring imperfections. Yet, they experienced God's amazing mercy and blossomed in the light of God's love.

WE ARE LOVED BY GOD

The first step toward intimacy comes when we understand that we, for all our imperfections, are loved by God and created by God and are integral to God's divine will for our families, our communities, and our world. "You are a child of the universe, / no less than the trees and the stars," writes Max Ehrmann in his classic poem "Desiderata" (© 1952).

reflections

FAITHFUL FRIENDS: WATCHING OVER ONE ANOTHER IN LOVE

Use this space to record thoughts, reflections, insights, prayer concerns, or other matters that arise from your weekly conversations with faithful friends.

— 3 —

Seeing God's Love in Others

PSALM FOR PRAYING

Psalm 36:5-7

Your steadfast love, O LORD, extends to the
    heavens,
    your faithfulness to the clouds.
Your righteousness is like the mighty
    mountains,
    your judgments are like the great deep;
    you save humans and animals alike,
        O LORD.
How precious is your steadfast love, O God!

DAILY READINGS

DAY ONE
John 15:9-17 *(Jesus' command to love one another)*

DAY TWO
Ruth 1:1-18 *(Naomi and Ruth)*

DAY THREE
Matthew 1:18-24 *(Mary and Joseph)*

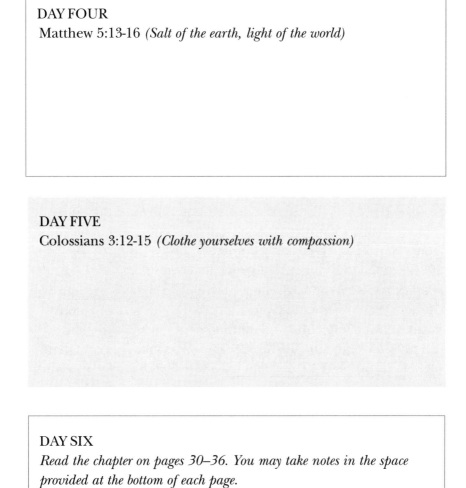

DAY FOUR

Matthew 5:13-16 *(Salt of the earth, light of the world)*

DAY FIVE

Colossians 3:12-15 *(Clothe yourselves with compassion)*

DAY SIX

Read the chapter on pages 30–36. You may take notes in the space provided at the bottom of each page.

UNTIL I MARRIED at the age of thirty-three, most of my friends and boyfriends had been people of faith, all deeply involved in their houses of worship. But when I met the man who would become my husband and soulmate, I was surprised and distressed to learn that he was not a churchgoer and that he was rather indifferent to the idea of forging a personal relationship with God. His mother had been an ordained minister, and Larry had attended church as a child. However, unlike my own parents, my in-laws stopped pressing their children to go to church once they left elementary school.

Larry and I were drawn to each other for the reasons that lovers are—we both had a boisterous sense of humor, liked the same music and movies, enjoyed travel, had learned important lessons from previous failed romances. And we both knew three weeks after meeting each other that we were meant to be partners in life.

However, from the beginning the "religion thing" was a hurdle. I couldn't remember a time in my life when I was not an enthusiastic and active churchgoer. I had sung in my church choir since I was five years old. Sundays for me had always centered on Sunday school, the worship service, and a big lunch with family or friends. I had always spent at least two or three weeknights in Bible study, attending choir practices or church meetings or participating in church-based projects—from prison ministry to voter registration to tutoring in an after-school program.

But Larry just wasn't interested. Even after we decided to get married, he refused to go to church. We never fought about it; it was just that he'd get caught up in some TV movie or ball game, or offer to do the grocery shopping while I was at church. Finally, I stopped asking him to accompany me. And by the time we'd been married three months, I found myself not wanting to leave him on

reflections

Sundays, so I'd sleep in or go shopping with him. Togetherness with my new husband became, for a while, more important than going to church. Before I realized it, I had been away from church for six months.

WORSHIP IN THE PARK

Because my faith—and my involvement in church—was such a defining element of my life, I was determined to find a way to get Larry in church. I fussed, demanded, bribed, and begged. Finally, however, I decided to "do" church in a different way. One beautiful spring Sunday, I got up early and packed a picnic brunch. I woke Larry and invited him to the park. We took along a boom box, Larry's favorite jazz CDs, and a candle. In the park, I lit the candle, turned on the music and said to my husband, "Tell me why you like baseball so much."

He eyed me suspiciously for just a second, detected no ulterior motive, and told the story. His father, who had died ten years before we met, loved baseball. Larry's fondest memories were of listening to his father talk about meeting Jackie Robinson and Willie Mays in person, trading baseball cards, and attending White Sox games, just the two of them in the early 1960s at Comiskey Park. My tough, streetwise husband actually cried as he told me how much he missed ball games with his father.

We sat in silence for a while. When Larry had collected himself, I unpacked the food and we ate. My husband then asked me about my love of church music. (The one or two times we had attended worship, he marveled that I knew most of the hymns by heart.) I told him about the first choir I was ever invited to join. I was five years old and Mrs. Mary Tolbert, our pastor's wife, had recruited

reflections

31

children to sing. She was the first person to tell me I had a pretty voice, and coaxed me to sing my first solo—"Lord, for Tomorrow." (I still know it by heart.)

As I told the story, I remembered anew that choir experience as a defining moment in my own life as a Christian and a church member. Mrs. Tolbert was one of the first adults outside my family to praise my talents and encourage church participation. She taught us that we were never too young or old to give ourselves to Jesus and to share with others. Larry watched me as I recalled singing with and being loved by Mrs. Tolbert, and he said, "No wonder you always sing like you love every word!"

The following Sunday, Larry was up before I was, ready to go to the park. We lit our candle and told each other more personal stories: secrets, joys, heartaches, hopes, and disappointments. After about five weeks of worship in the park, Larry confessed that he had learned more about me on our Sundays together than in all the time we had dated. It was then that I told him about a place where friends met regularly to tell their stories, share their joys, and bear one another's burdens: "It's called *church*."

Although my husband at first could not imagine making himself that vulnerable before anyone, the deep intimacy we found together during our Sundays in the park opened his heart and mind. Two months later, after visiting several churches, we became members of Hobson United Methodist Church, where he joined a devastatingly honest Sunday school class for recovering alcoholics. He became a leader in our ministries with homeless men. As he shared his life and story with others, I could see his self-love and self-acceptance increase. I rejoiced to watch him grow from having only one other intimate friendship—with his brother—to finding close friendships with several persons from our church.

reflections

32

Beyond Larry's joining church, the ironic thing about our worship adventures in the park is that I have never considered myself a strong witness to the faith. I was always afraid of coming on too strong or being too preachy. I'd invite friends and co-workers to attend our Sunday church services, and I made sure I welcomed visitors to our congregation. However, telling my story as an expression of my Christian discipleship has never been "my thing."

At the same time, though, if you ask friends and family to name my strengths, they'll probably say that I'm a good listener, that nurturing relationships with others is the most important aspect of my life, and that I am always willing to say what I think and what I feel. That's what Larry and I shared during our Sundays in the park—our witness. We both found ourselves spiritually stronger and our marriage richer because of that time together.

CHRISTIAN CHARACTER IN CONTEXT

"Friendship at its deepest level is always risky and scary," writes James B. Nelson, a theologian and author of *The Intimate Connection: Male Sexuality, Masculine Spirituality* (The Westminster Press, 1988; page 52). "I have to have a fairly firm grip on myself to let go of myself. If I don't know who I really am . . . I will be afraid to open myself to the intense influences of intimacy."

For some of us who are blessed with enough to eat, safe living conditions, healthy and happy families, and uncomplicated friendships, it may be hard to understand the idea of "risks" in our intimate relationships. Many of us, though, have been broken and betrayed by people we should have been able to trust. Or we have lived so long with the message of unworthiness of love from God or anyone else that we have erected emotional fences to protect

reflections

33

ourselves. In Alice Walker's Pulitzer Prize-winning novel *The Color Purple* (Harcourt Brace Jovanovich, 1982), Celie, the main character, has been abused all her life by men. Finally, she's had enough. She stops writing in her diary to God, who she figures is "just like all the other mens I know. Trifling, forgitful and lowdown." She

Intimacy is seeing the love of God in one another.

tells her friend, Shug, "[God] give me a lynched daddy, a crazy mama, a lowdown dog of a step pa and a sister I probably won't ever see again....If he ever listened to poor colored women the world would be a different place, I can tell you" (pages 199–200).

When Shug encourages Celie to look for God, not as a man but in rocks, flowers, trees, or the color purple, Celie tries. But her anger and sense of betrayal threaten to overwhelm her. "Every time I conjure up a rock, I throw it," she says (page 204).

As we invite and are invited into intimate relationships, we must remember that our shared stories include tales of pain, violence, disappointment, death, and despair. In revealing all of who we are, we risk being seen as not worth loving. However, the call to intimacy includes the promise that God's love is wide enough to cover both our joys and our sufferings. Embarking on relationships with others, we also are promising to love, to listen, and to embrace others, through whatever sorrows or joys each of us carries.

Each week in our congregation, we sing a song of greeting to one another in which we celebrate being together again, each of us a holy child of God. The song is a reminder that once we accept that we are living testimonies to God's astonishing love and grace, the logical and desired next step is to find communion and connection with others. People with whom we have our closest, deepest

reflections

relationships are those who, like God, have seen us at our worst and still love us. They know our stories. They are the ones who kick up their heels with us when we are glad, cheer us on in our moments of triumph, tell us hard truths when we need to hear them, and hold our hands in times of sorrow.

SHINING TOGETHER

Intimate relationships at their best are those in which we risk and make ourselves vulnerable to our friends, family, lovers, or members of our faith communities and church school classmates. *Intimacy* by definition means trusting others with our stories, ambitions, fears, and hopes. In fact, biblical stories of friendship are often cast as covenants, promises of loyalty, and relationships in the name of God. Although the relationships between mothers- and daughters-in-law have jokingly become icons for acrimony, Ruth pledged loyalty to her mother-in-law, Naomi (Ruth 1:16-17); and the two of them trusted one another and worked together to assure their financial security and Ruth's romantic future.

It comes down to this: Intimacy is seeing the love of God in one another. When Jesus declares us to be light, he also calls us to see God's light in others, so that we shine together to illuminate the dark corners of loneliness, despair, and isolation. Our connections with one another are not only good for our own souls; they are tangible manifestations of God's love for us and our relationship with God through Jesus Christ.

As translated by Eugene Petersen in THE MESSAGE, Matthew 5:14-16 reminds us: "You're here to be light, bringing out the God-colors in the world. God is not a secret to be kept. We're going public with this, as public as a city on a hill. If I make you light-

reflections

bearers, you don't think I'm going to hide you under a bucket, do you? I'm putting you on a light stand. Now that I've put you there on a hilltop, on a light stand—shine! Keep open house; be generous with your lives. By opening up to others, you'll prompt people to open up with God. . . ." (From THE MESSAGE. Copyright © Eugene Peterson, 1993, 1994, 1995. Used by permission of NavPress Publishing Group.)

reflections

FAITHFUL FRIENDS: WATCHING OVER ONE ANOTHER IN LOVE

Use this space to record thoughts, reflections, insights, prayer concerns, or other matters that arise from your weekly conversations with faithful friends.

— 4 —

Connecting With
a Community of Faith

Psalm 84:1-2, 4

How lovely is your dwelling place,
   O LORD of hosts!
My soul longs, indeed it faints
   for the courts of the LORD;
my heart and my flesh sing for joy
   to the living God.

. . .

happy are those who live in your house,
   ever singing your praise.

DAILY READINGS

DAY ONE

Genesis 37 *(Joseph and his brothers)*

DAY TWO

Matthew 11:25-30 *(All who are weary, come)*

DAY THREE

John 4:7-29 *(The Samaritan woman at the well)*

DAY FOUR
Leviticus 19:1-18 *(Life in God's community)*

DAY FIVE
Galatians 6:1-10 *(Work for the good of all)*

DAY SIX
Read the chapter on pages 42–47. You may take notes in the space provided at the bottom of each page.

THE CONGREGATION I ATTEND averages 75 to 100 in worship on Sunday. At least 40 percent of our members are either at some stage of recovery from—or are still addicted to—drugs or alcohol. Each week, at the start of worship, we celebrate those having birthdays and anniversaries in the coming week. It's not unusual during this time for a woman or man to rise and invite the congregation to celebrate a *re*-birth day. For example, last week, we cheered a man celebrating the six weeks he had gone without smoking crack, the longest "clean" time he had achieved in ten years. One woman was marking ten years without a drink. Yet another woman asked us to sing a blessing/prayer original to our congregation ("Bless Her Life, Lord") to commemorate the day five years ago when she walked away from an abusive marriage.

Most new members and visitors are taken aback by such raw honesty and the congregation's willingness to discuss these issues openly in the context of worship. Many of us were reared to keep our troubles to ourselves. As a child, I heard rumors in my very proper, very traditional congregation about someone's aunt who was addicted to prescription drugs, or the usher's son who was mentally ill, or our lay leader's spouse who had been fired from a teaching job for drinking. But such information was not openly acknowledged in Sunday school class or at Bible study, and it was surely not detailed as a prayer request.

Many of us were reared to keep our troubles to ourselves.

In the church I attend today, which is located in the heart of the inner city, most of our members—including our key leaders—live in public housing, have very modest incomes, and regularly

reflections

42

endure the public humiliation that comes from having to use food stamps, depend on free school lunches, and contend with the criminal and juvenile justice systems. Any modesty and self-consciousness about sharing their troubles has been compromised, because they have to tell their story publicly to welfare workers, police officers, and bill collectors just to survive. They are looking for at least that much honesty in their faith community. They don't want to have to "front," or put on a different face. Instead, they have helped re-create our faith community as a place where we can find compassion, forgiveness, empathy, strength when we need it, and a shoulder to cry on when we need that, too.

CHRISTIAN CHARACTER IN COMMUNITY

Intimacy in the Christian community should mean that wherever we are gathered is a safe and open place, where we can herald our smallest accomplishments or ask for prayer and support in our loneliest and most fear-filled hours. It shouldn't be the place where we fear "telling our business." It should be the spiritual home where we can lay our burdens at God's feet and at the altar of God's love; and the people who say they are sisters and brothers in the faith should meet us there to pray, weep, rejoice, and ponder us.

Stark honesty can evoke holy moments. We find in my congregation that it is our willingness to engage one another at our weakest that makes us stronger as witnesses to the power of Christ to heal. One Sunday, we were visited by an adult Sunday school class from an affluent suburban church that sometimes works as a partner in ministry with others. After several of our members had asked for prayers for their struggles with drug addiction, one of our visitors

reflections

43

stood. She was well-dressed and obviously well off. She trembled as she spoke without preamble:

"I want to ask this church to pray for me," she said, tears running down her cheeks. "I've never said this out loud in any church; but I just can't stop drinking, and it's about to ruin my marriage and my family. I need your help."

She began to weep and could say no more. Somewhere, one of the homeless guys from our church shouted, "Amen!" And one of our teens—a refugee from foster care—got out of his seat and went over to hug her. The members of her own Sunday school class were stunned. Their congregation is wonderful, and they use their resources in ministries that help many in our city who are hurting and oppressed. Still, at least for one member, the church had not yet become a place where a well-heeled leader could safely admit aloud that she had a drinking problem and trust her class members and fellow leaders to offer her support and acceptance.

Was it her congregation that restrained her from being honest? Maybe. Even the most loving among us sometimes get stuck in the notion of church as only being meaningful when there is quiet prayer, reflective music, and lecture-toned preaching. Otherwise, we purse our lips and radiate silent waves of disapproval if someone says, "Amen!" a little too loudly, sings "The Old Rugged Cross" a little too robustly, or cries audibly during the morning prayer. Too many of us still play the tapes in our heads that say, "Respectable people keep their personal problems to themselves."

STRENGTH IN VULNERABILITY

After we joined our church, I remember the Sunday my husband admitted to the congregation that he was an alcoholic and

reflections

needed their prayers and their support. He got up without warning during the altar call, stood at the microphone, and told his story.

I was mortified. I'd always fancied myself as a woman with her act together. I didn't mind being part of a tell-it-like-it-is church as long I was the one reaching out, giving the hugs, and helping others in trouble. But my husband's public admission was a turning point for me. For the first time, my private life and family struggles were laid bare. But what I found in the aftermath was release. Friends called to say, "I'm praying for you." People who saw us as the formidable and unapproachable "perfect couple" engaged us as friends. And several women friends and I started a Sunday school class for women living with an addicted spouse or family member.

> **It is in risk and vulnerability that we have found God-graced communion with others.**

Of course, this idea of revealing our vulnerability and weakness runs counter to our secular notions of putting up an I've-got-it-all-together front, of power found in strength, of stoicism as the best expression of responsible living. However, throughout the history of our faith, it is in risk and vulnerability that we have found true God-graced communion with others. Joseph, after being sold into slavery by his brothers, endured hardships, found favor in the sight of his boss (who, in fact, liked Joseph's truth-telling), and was put in charge of rationing food during a time of famine. When his brothers, who didn't recognize him, came before him to ask for aid, Joseph ultimately embraced them, empathized with their struggles, and shared his good fortune with them (Genesis 42–45).

reflections

The Samaritan woman did not find condemnation at the well. Rather, she encountered a Messiah who wanted to know her story and who talked with her about faith and real life. He shattered her image of all Jews as Samaritan-hating chauvinists who would not even drink from the same fountain as a woman like her. Jesus was not put off by her ancestry, her gender (remember, in those days you didn't talk theology with women), or her reputation.

Joseph, upon learning that his fiancée, Mary, was pregnant, planned to call off their marriage quietly to save face (hers and his own). But after being confronted by a messenger from heaven, Joseph put faith before fear and kept his promise (Matthew 1:18-24). It probably was not easy. The Bible doesn't tell us much about how it happened, but most of us watch enough talk shows to imagine what friends and family must have said when Joseph told them, "I never had sex with Mary, and she's never cheated on me, but she's pregnant and it's God's kid." At best, Joseph endured ridicule from his friends, and Mary was called a few harsh names. But by trusting his relationship with God, trusting Mary, and risking his reputation for the sake of faithful obedience, Joseph became earthly father to the greatest person in the history of the world.

INTIMATE COMMUNITIES OF FAITH

When we are church at our very best, we find sweet communion with other children of God who have good days and bad days, family joys and family sorrows, personal triumphs and personal tragedies. Jesus admonished his followers to love one another and bear one another's burdens. His words invite us to establish relationships beyond the barriers of pride, isolation, and the modern-day commandment to "mind your own business." Rather, we are

reflections

called to connect with others in such a way that we know their birthdays and their "re-birth" days.

We are invited to build relationships of trust and mutual respect, so that on the 27th we invite to dinner that friend whose disability check doesn't stretch to cover the last week of the month—and the friend is welcomed as a friend, not a charity case. When we experience true intimacy in our Christian communities, we not only accept church friends' offerings of casseroles and cakes when a loved one dies, but we can feel safe asking for prayer by phone in the middle of the day while our bosses are meeting to decide whether or not to lay off a hundred workers. When we build a Christian fellowship where we practice openness and expect healing, we can admit out loud that we struggle with alcohol, languish in foster care, worry about money, feel stuck in loveless marriages—and still meet faithful Christian friends who stand ready to walk with us through the valley of the shadow.

Intimate communities of faith should be places where we can be authentic and vulnerable and open before the God who loves us unconditionally, in communion with others who can testify from personal experience that Jesus is a rock in a weary land. The value of true Christian community is that we are always welcomed home, whether we bring riches and joys, or battle scars and sorrows.

reflections

47

FAITHFUL FRIENDS: WATCHING OVER ONE ANOTHER IN LOVE

Use this space to record thoughts, reflections, insights, prayer concerns, or other matters that arise from your weekly conversations with faithful friends.

— 5 —

Practicing Intimacy as a Spiritual Discipline

PSALM FOR PRAYING

Psalm 63:1-4

O God, you are my God, I seek you,
    my soul thirsts for you;
my flesh faints for you,
    as in a dry and weary land where there is
        no water.
So I have looked upon you in the sanctuary,
    beholding your power and glory.
Because your steadfast love is better than life,
    my lips will praise you.
So I will bless you as long as I live;
    I will lift up my hands and call on your
        name.

DAILY READINGS

DAY ONE
Matthew 5:38-48 *(Love your neighbor, love your enemies)*

DAY TWO
Matthew 25:31-40 *(Jesus teaches, "As you did it to one of the least . . . you did it to me")*

DAY THREE
1 John 4:7-12 *(Love is from God)*

DAY FOUR
Philippians 4:4-7 *(Don't worry about anything)*

DAY FIVE
Hebrews 13:1-6 *(Let mutual love continue)*

DAY SIX
Read the chapter on pages 52–57. You may take notes in the space provided at the bottom of each page.

WE LIVE IN A WORLD WHERE the call to love our neighbor has been replaced with such adages as "fences make good neighbors," "keep your business to yourself," and "familiarity breeds contempt." Of course, these sayings become popular because there are some truths tucked in between the lines. Who hasn't had a neighbor or family member who became notorious for dropping by without calling? And we all know co-workers or church members who are so nosey that we dread even casual conversations with them. I had a roommate in undergraduate school who liked to borrow my clothes—even underwear!

Sometimes, however, the fear of being overrun by people who don't have appropriate boundaries renders us incapable of nurturing intimate friendships, family relationships, and ties to our faith communities. As we get older, it gets harder for many of us to make new friends, largely because we have internalized the message that closeness equals smothering. In the last few months, several of my friends have stopped attending church, complaining that the church "expects too much."

Caring for yourself gives you the "juice" you need to reach out to others.

When I probed further, I discovered that "too much" included being asked to find a prayer partner in the congregation and talk to that person once a week.

"I have my own friends and I'm an introvert," one friend told me. "I don't want to be forced to meet new people."

It has surprised me to learn this late in life that I am something of an introvert myself. I have a demanding job that often requires

reflections

me to be "on" for days at a time. I recently conducted Bible study for a gathering of seven thousand women, and I think five thousand of them wanted to talk with me personally. It was extremely gratifying, and I met some wonderful people.

However, when I got home from the conference, I was irritable and tired. I turned off my phone for five days. I didn't talk to a soul or leave my house. When my pastor called asking me to be on a church committee, I almost bit his head off! What I realized is that I need space and time away from my job. As a result, I'm learning to schedule quality time with friends and family, finding time to try new things and make new friends; in the process I am discovering that I have to be as committed to my non-work relationships as I am to my job.

THE DISCIPLINE OF INTIMACY

Making time for relationships with others is part of my discipline of intimacy. This discipline includes showing love to other children of God, connecting to the Christ in others (through church, community ties, and social action), worshiping God together, and nurturing relationships with friends and family. To practice intimacy as a spiritual discipline, consider these suggestions:

(1) Let your first prayer of the day be one of gratitude for God's abiding love, and a promise to model that love for others. I use the simple prayer, "Day by Day," from the musical *Godspell,* asking for greater awareness in seeing, loving, and following God in all I do that day. Instead of beginning your prayer time by petitioning God, you might start by giving thanks that you are created by God and loved by God. And vow to connect to the light of God in others.

reflections

53

(2) Include tangible expressions of self-love and self-care on your day's "to-do" list. Set the clock an hour earlier and go for a walk. Turn off the TV one hour earlier in the evening and read something uplifting. Take ten minutes of your lunch hour and give thanks. Keep sabbath by cooking Sunday supper on Saturday night and then spending Sunday afternoon playing board games with family or friends. Keep your after-Sunday-worship spirit alive by avoiding the mall or the laundromat until Monday. Take your elderly mother, aunt, grandmother, or neighbor out for a pedicure, or brush their hair while they tell you a story from their younger days. Extend the same courtesies to yourself. An angry, harried, burned-out Christian is not likely to have much to offer in terms of intimate relationships. Caring for yourself gives you the "juice" you need to reach out to others. A shining, well-loved spirit is contagious. Cultivate your own.

(3) Connect each day with one person who loves you. Nothing I do, no bad attitude I conjure, no whining complaint I make can stand up to my mother's loving, "can-do" disposition. We talk at least every other day, and just the sound of her voice makes me glad to be alive and part of the human race. I get the same feeling when I talk to my best friend, Toni. When my husband was alive, he would call five times a day to say, "I love you." Your love and care mean that much to someone in your life. By talking regularly with people who love you and champion the things you do, you may find yourself being more loving to others and actually practicing intimacy.

(4) Regularly practice acts of justice, mercy, and reconciliation. A few years ago, I was in a particularly stressful job with a boss who seemed to second-guess and mistrust my every move. Between my

reflections

54

anger and resentment, his mistrust, and my staff's fear of being phased out, I was coming undone. During Lent, however, my pastor advised us to take on something new instead of giving up something. So I decided to pray daily for my boss during Lent. To be honest, the first day of my Lenten prayer was done with great effort. However, as I delved into Scriptures about mercy, kindness, and walking a mile in another person's shoes, I started to pray for my boss's happiness and well-being. I prayed for a close relative of his who was terminally ill. Whenever I learned that he was going to make a presentation about our work, I prayed that he would be well received. A funny thing happened. As I prayed for him over those weeks, I

> **Practicing intimacy . . . all it requires is that we take the time to see the love of God in those we meet.**

found myself answering him more pleasantly and responding with less venom (even though his questions were still annoying). By Easter, my soul was quieter; and I really did wish in my soul that my boss would find peace himself. It wasn't a miraculous transformation; it was just that, once I really understood that my boss was also a well-loved child of God, it became harder to be angry with him. How are you integrating love for yourself and others with the pursuit of meaningful relationships in your prayer life? Do you reach out to individuals even as you try to address such issues as hunger, poverty, public housing, voter registration, and disaster response? By praying for and connecting with individuals in times of trouble—even if the trouble is of their own making—you are practicing intimacy along with mercy and justice.

_____

_____

_____

_____

_____

reflections

*(5) **Keep an intimacy journal.*** Jot down song lyrics, poems, and good things people say to you. Paste in drawings by your children and grandchildren, tickets from a movie that moved you, or clippings from newspapers—anything that reminds you that God loves you and calls you to love others. Set a goal of adding at least two or three new items a week. Bring your journal to Bible study or Sunday school, and discuss the contents with others. You'll be surprised at how much inspiration you can find in everyday life for loving yourself and others, and you'll learn that God's love for us all is manifest daily in our life and work and in our connections with our family, friends, and communities.

*(6) **Say "please," "thank you," and "good job" to strangers.*** I am old enough to lament the good old days when customer service included coherent sales clerks and service with a smile. I hate going to fast-food restaurants, because I am faced with too many sullen teens who don't acknowledge my presence, let alone smile. However, I have also witnessed customers who bark their orders as if talking to robots, not to children of God. I find that if I ask, "How are you?" of the checkout worker, or say, "Thanks for helping me," to the bank teller, I am often met with surprised looks and sudden smiles. Although I live in an urban area, I say hello to strangers in the line in the grocery store, and I give up my seat to older adults on the bus or subway. Each time I do, I find that the people I'm kind to are kind in return. I like to think that I have reminded them of their beauty as a child of God, and I hope a glimmer of God's love has shone through me in that moment.

Practicing intimacy—does it sound silly? Does it feel like a lot of work? It's not really. All it requires is that we take the time to see

reflections

the love of God in those we meet; that we exchange useless worry and irritability for prayer-filled faith; and that we say out loud by our words and actions that being part of God's community of faith makes a wonderful difference in how we live and move and have our being.

reflections

FAITHFUL FRIENDS: WATCHING OVER ONE ANOTHER IN LOVE

Use this space to record thoughts, reflections, insights, prayer concerns, or other matters that arise from your weekly conversations with faithful friends.

— 6 —

Planning the Next Steps Together

Psalm 67:1-3

May God be gracious to us and bless us
  and make his face to shine upon us,
that your way may be known upon earth,
  your saving power among all nations.
Let the peoples praise you, O God;
  let all the peoples praise you.

FOR THE PAST FEW WEEKS you have experienced the "Come and See" portion of this study, exploring aspects of the Christian character trait of intimacy. You have learned about and reflected upon "Knowing Who You Are—And Whose You Are," "Seeing God's Love in Others," "Connecting With a Community of Faith," and "Practicing Intimacy as a Spiritual Discipline." You have experienced psalms for praying and lectio divina to engage Scripture in a prayerful way. You have communicated regularly as faithful friends with another person in the group. You have learned all this in the company of other Christians who also seek God's "good life."

In the following space, take some time now to write about particular learnings from the previous sessions that have been meaningful or significant to you.

The time has come to move from understanding intimacy to developing practices of intimacy. It is time to "Go and Do" intimacy in your group.

At your next session, you and your group will plan together how to "try out" what you have learned about the Christian character trait of intimacy. Then, for the weeks to follow, you will put your plan into action, both as individuals and as a group.

Your group planning session will be most effective if each member, in preparation for the session, takes a few minutes to brainstorm ways in which the group can begin to practice intimacy over the next six weeks during the "Go and Do" portion of the study.

On the pages that follow, you will see several boxes, each of which contains an idea prompt. These idea prompts are designed to help you imagine ways in which you and your group could put into practice what you have learned about intimacy. Allow your mind to explore every possible avenue for embodying this notion of intimacy in your life as a Christian. Resist the tendency to edit your ideas; instead, record all of them in the spaces provided. Be ready to share them with the group when you meet.

As you consider and record your ideas, keep in mind that ideas are only a part of Christian character. Christianity comes alive only when, inspired by ideas, we move into the world, practicing and embodying our faith. That's when we truly become the body of Christ and begin—haltingly at first but then with confidence and faith—living the good life together.

Lectio divina Scripture passages

Behavioral changes to make

Ministry events to consider

Mission work to conceive and implement

Speakers to invite

Field trips, retreats, pilgrimages to take

Books to read, movies to see

Other ideas

ACKNOWLEDGMENTS

Living the Good Life Together: A Study of Christian Character in Community is the result of a very good idea. The idea was that the church needed help in teaching God's people to cultivate patterns or practices of holy living—in other words, to learn to live a good life as defined by Scripture and exemplified by Jesus. This idea became the subject of a very fruitful conversation, thanks especially to the participation of Timothy W. Whitaker, Resident Bishop of the Florida Annual Conference of The United Methodist Church; L. Gregory Jones, Dean and Professor of Theology at Duke University Divinity School; and Paul W. Chilcote, Professor of Historical Theology and Wesleyan Studies at Asbury Theological Seminary in Florida. Their commitment to the idea and their contributions to the development process provided the vision and the impetus for this unique resource.